Nature and Maine Hunter Communicate

By

Edmond Theriault

First published January 2017 (MMXVII)

© Copyright   Theriault's Snowshoes, Brian J. Theriault

Soft cover: ISBN   9780991006922

EBook: ISBN   9780991006939

All Rights Reserved

No portion of this publication may be produced, stored in any electronic system, or transmitted in any form or by any means, electronic, mechanical, photocopy, recording, or otherwise, without written permission from the author, Edmond Theriault, or the publisher: Brian J. Theriault.

Brian J. Theriault

P.O. Box 242

Fort Kent Mills, Maine 04744 U.S.A

theriaultsnowshoes@gmail.com

ilovesnowshoes.com

SK1-664

SP0022000

Publisher: Brian J. Theriault

Editor& Diagrams: Edmond Theriault

Technical Assistance: Benjamin Latvis

Cover picture & Back picture & Photographs: Brian J. Theriault

Cover & Back design: Tracey Hartt

Aroostook County, Maine, USA

Printed in the United States of America

DEDICATION

This book is dedicated to the family of Joseph Theriault and Eva Babin Theriault, and their children: Elmer, Eli, Alban, Edmond, Lillian, Stanley, Lorianne, Kathleen, Alire (Pete), Ethel, Gloria, Rita, Inez, Donald, and Ronald Theriault, an orphan who was brought up as one of the family.

Joseph and Eva Theriault

This is a photo of me and my siblings from 1994...
L-R front Rita, Ethel, Lori, Kate, Lil, Inez, Gloria... L-R back Ron, Pete, Eli, Edmond, Al, Don

CONTENTS

Chapter 1	The Beginning of a Hunter	page 6
Chapter 2	Short Hunting Stories	page 9
Chapter 3	Hector Long Story	page 25
Chapter 4	Tips and Things About Hunting	page 26
Chapter 5	A Moose Hunt	page 37
Chapter 6	Philippine Hunt	page 39
Chapter 7	Porky	page 40
Chapter 8	Partridges	page 41
Chapter 9	A Chilling Warning	page 42
	Hunting Tools	page 44
	Venison Mincemeat Pie Recipe	page 45
	About the Author	page 46

Chapter 1

The Beginning of a Hunter

I remember the great depression, when most people had no jobs and no money. I came from a family of fourteen children. My dad was a hunter, a fisherman, and a trapper; and I wanted to be like him. I grew up knowing that hunting was necessary for survival, so when my dad asked me to go rabbit hunting, I was ready.

I was about ten years old at that time. I remember the rabbits had turned white and there was no snow on the ground. Maybe that was not fair for the rabbit, but it was very good for us. My dad would make me run to bush piles and bunches of grasses while he stayed in the road. When I would start a rabbit, he would shoot it as it crossed the road. At that time, I didn't know that beagles did that.

When I was about twelve years old, my dad showed me how to safely operate a 410 shot gun. He warned me to never point a gun at anything unless I wanted to shoot it. He showed me how to aim and not to waste any ammunition, since it cost money. The next time we went hunting, I carried that 410. I knew what my job was. I traveled along the side of the road looking for rabbits. Looking underneath the trees, there was an old log on the ground. And on the other side of that log, a partridge was looking at me. I could see its head and part of its neck. I was shaking as I prepared to shoot. That was the first time I was shooting any weapon, but I had not been told what would really happen. The head disappeared. I lay the gun on the ground and ran to the log and jumped over it. Before I hit the ground, I saw a partridge flapping its wings and jumping around and a whole covey of partridge watching it. When they saw me, they tried to take off, but wings were hitting the branches, and I was trying to catch them with my bare hands. There must have been eight or nine of them. My dad came over and I told him what had happened. He said the next time you fire a gun, the first thing you do is reload. You want to be ready in case you need to shoot again. He explained that the target could have just been wounded. My dad always pointed out that it was important to be accurate so your targeted animal would suffer the shortest amount of time. He knew that animals reproduced more than the land could support, so his family survived. He also stressed that it was easy to get lost in the woods and how to keep track of the directions you were moving and the way the main roads were placed. The lessons continued until I graduated from high school and left for the military service.

The white tailed deer started moving into Northern Maine when the virgin forests were being cut in the early nineteen hundreds. The caribous had migrated out and never came back. Farming and wood cutting gave the deer all they needed to increase their numbers. In the early days of lumbering, many horses were used, and feeding them required many fields for hay and oats. The deer kept increasing.

I remember in the 1940s, in the early spring, when the snow in the woods had not yet melted, the hungry deer would come out in the open fields to feed. In fields in Portage, Maine, and along Route 161, you could, in some fields, count up to a hundred deer. There were deer in almost every field, and that was in the daytime. I don't know if there were more at night.

A game preserve was started east of Route 161, past Guerette. It did not take many years before it had to be abandoned. The deer had killed all the trees that had been feeding them in the winter.

Now with bucks only laws, I have not hunted deer for about forty years. That is about the time the coyotes moved in. We are told the shortage of deer is caused by the hard winters. After 90 years, I do not remember any easy winters. I believe the state is just producing enough deer in Northern Maine to feed the coyotes.

Every year a new hunting season comes and plans have to be made. The main reason I am writing about my adventures in the woods is to show the hunters of today how it was for me at that time. It covers from the time I came back from the military service in 1947, to about 1980, when the coyotes started cleaning every living thing in our woods, except the moose.

When I returned after four and a half years in the service, I was exposed to deer hunting. After a few trips in the woods where I found deer tracks everywhere and plenty of rubs and scratches, I decided I would wait for the snows. I could tell what was going on. I really wanted to get the oldest buck after the rutting season. To accomplish that, I had to be able to see the biggest track. I had a lot to learn and many surprises.

Lew Gervais and I have been hunting friends since grammar school. In winter, we hunted rabbits on snowshoes. Almost all of our Saturdays were spent chasing rabbits. That is probably the reason why we thought it was funny when we went in the military service. Everyone had a ten minute break every hour walking on solid ground. I always used my father's snowshoes, and Lew had a pair of snowshoes made by Willie Roy, a relative. (Willie Roy is the snowshoe maker who taught me how to make snowshoes before he retired.)

Chapter 2

Short Hunting Stories

This hunting experience took place in about 1947 at the end of the hunting season. I am writing it as a warning about what can happen in Northern Maine. My friend Lew Gervais, with his uncle Albert Roy and a Lozier neighbor, had planned a hunting week by Blue River Canada, where you cross into Maine at the Pierre Landry camps on Dead Brook. It was past the middle of November with about 6 inches of snow on the ground. When they invited me to join them, I accepted. Everything was arranged. So on that Sunday afternoon, we moved into the camp about 3 miles from the main camp on Dead Brook. The snow had formed a crust. As you put your weight on it, the crust would break, making noise and making the going hard. We spent a good week hunting, getting one nice buck and a smaller spike. When Saturday came, we were running out of food. We decided to stay a few more days to hunt. We would send two of the party to get some food. On Saturday, Lew had killed a rabbit, so I made a stew for Sunday. The only addition to the stew was two small onions and salt and pepper. We ate all of it. On Sunday afternoon, two hunters from Fort Kent arrived, Willard Pelletier and his brother-in-law Deprey. They were looking for a place to stay while they hunted. We told them we would be leaving by Monday night, so they could stay and take over the camp. They decided to sleep at camp and in the morning, go and get what they would need at Blue River. The surprise came in the morning. We got up to find that about thirty inches of snow had fallen during the night. There was snow above our knees, and we had no snowshoes. We were also surprised when we found that two deer had crossed the road about a hundred yards from our camp. They were traveling single file and making a canal with their bodies about eight inches deep. Lew and I decided to give chase to see if we could overtake those deer. After about an hour, we were getting tired and not getting closer. So we decided to go back. We were missing our old snowshoes.

Back at camp, our partners had tied the two vehicles together tight and found some two inch planks and made some kind of a plow in front of the first vehicle.

We started to try to open the road. The two vehicles would push the snow about ten to fifteen feet and back off so two of us would shovel the snow off the road. We were not making much progress, but we kept on until one of the vehicles broke down. We called for a conference to decide what we should do. It was about three o'clock in the afternoon, and we were very hungry. I was the only one who wanted to cut some deer steak and eat and wait until morning. The others wanted to start walking out immediately. They were saying it was illegal to eat deer meat in wood camps. I did not know that, and I did not care. Since all the others wanted to leave immediately, they won. Their reasoning was that there was no traffic of any kind on the road we were on and there were no piles of wood anywhere. They were saying that it was possible the company would not open the road that winter.

I called my friend Lew and told him that the others did not know how hard it was moving through the snow without snowshoes. I took the lead, breaking trail, and Lew followed me. I had gone about one mile when Lew asked to break trail. We had not seen the others for some time, and it was getting dark. Lew passed in front and I followed. After a short period of time, I noticed Lew was having a rough time. I told him to let me lead since I could not carry him. After about a mile, Lew asked if he could lie down and rest a while. I slowed down to let the others catch up to us since I wanted to stay close to Lew. Our other partners caught up with us. I explained that I wanted to watch Lew. I was really surprised to find out that the others could not break trail. They would take a few short steps, and want to rest. They were changing the lead position, but I was getting cold. Lew was last in line and, at times, we could not even see him. I told the others that I would try to go ahead and send someone to help them. Around the main camp, the good size trees had been cut. So when I made the last turn, I could not see anyone from our party. But in front, I could see the light from the main camp. Just seeing the light gave all of them a shot of energy, including me. Even Lew, who had not been seen for a while, caught up. All the people at the main camp were friendly and helpful. The cook had a feast for us in no time. Since all of us were so hungry, I wondered what we should devour first. I took a large bowl of the best soup I had ever eaten and gave the same to Lew. Once we downed the soup, we were not hungry anymore.

The bulldozer operator had cleared the area around the camp and gave us the good news; his job for the next day was to open the Dead Brook Road we were stuck on. When morning came, we followed the dozer for an easy 3 mile walk. Coming home I asked Lew what had happened to his snowshoes. He said that he did not know. And I did not know what had happened to my father's. I now believe this trip planted the seed that snowshoes will always be needed and I should be the one to carry on the tradition of making snowshoes for as long as possible. I have now made snowshoes for forty years, and my son Brian is left to carry on the tradition.

Now I will move on to some of the good size bucks I have harvested. Of course, you have to be able to shoot accurately and save your ammunition; and as my father warned me, don't get lost. Here in Northern Maine there are two north-south highways Route 11 and 161. With a good compass and a watch, you should have no problem. If you really want to be safe, bring 3 compasses. With only two, if they don't give you the same direction, you don't know which one is working.

To be a good hunter, you have to be able to shoot well and be accurate. Almost all my deer hunting has been done with open sight rifles. This is how I practiced: making sure the rifle is not loaded, I would bring my sights on a distant target as quickly as possible, pull the trigger, reload, and move on to a second target. After a few dry runs, I tried one or two practices using live ammunition, the rifle sights, and checking the targets. I believe in practicing a short time and more often. This accustoms you to handling your rifle. When you are shooting at a running deer, you have to put all your concentration on the exact spot where you want to hit that deer. The more familiar you are with a rifle, the easier that is going to be. You do not have time to use the gun sights.

The greatest danger in Northern Maine is getting lost. Having a map of the area you are going to hunt is helpful. Having a compass can save you much time, if you can use it. Using the sun and the North Star at night can be aides in case the compass goes wrong. Having two compasses is no help since you will not know which one is wrong. In the old days, when horses hauled the wood out, you could be quite sure they hauled going downhill, but now with the mechanization, you can't depend on that.

In Northern Maine, in Fort Kent, there are two roads going south, Route 161 and Route 11. All the lakes empty to the north in the Fish or St. John Rivers. The brooks are different; they can flow in any direction to the lakes or thoroughfares. About 39 miles south of Fort Kent, you will find some brooks and streams that flow south and some that flow north. Sometimes they can be short distances from each other.

My first big buck was a big surprise. Hunting along an old woods road with thick young firs and spruces growing on one side of the road, I heard for the first time what I thought was a fawn bleating. I saw a doe run across the road, so I did not move. Nothing was happening, so I started imitating, as well as I could, the bleating I had heard. It did not take long before I got an answer, and it was coming towards me through the thick firs and bleating regularly while I kept silent. There was a light crust on the snow and I could not see, but I could tell he was coming towards me at a fast pace. I prepared my 30.30 Winchester, and none too early. Less than 10 feet away from me, antlers were bursting out of the thick firs. I fired and that buck took one leap and landed about 3 feet from me. By the bleating, I was expecting a fawn and I would not have shot. Instead, I had the biggest deer I had ever seen. The buck had flat antlers with eight points. The

work began. The entrails came out. I saved the liver and the heart. I started pulling the deer out. That day I had hunted in between Cross Lake and Square Lake area, where the land is quite level, making dragging easier. Once the deer was home, we were in no hurry to prepare the meat for the freezer.

After a hunt, I always go over what happened and if I could have done something better. This time, I believe that when I bleated, this buck thought I was another buck after his doe, and he was coming to fight me. I won.

Greatly encouraged by my first deer hunt, the next year, I planned to hunt in the Nixon area. That large area is south of Winterville, where there is a Nixon Railroad Siding, where lumber can be shipped out. One of my father's friends, Gilbert Godin, had a wood camp where he worked with his sons. I knew I could stay overnight and borrow a horse if I needed one to get the deer out.

On my first day, I visited different areas to see what direction the bucks were moving. In the afternoon, I started following a big buck. He was moving towards a bunch of thick, smaller trees. As I approached slowly, I could hear animals moving, but I could see nothing. The big buck I was following was somewhere in there, so I waited. The sky was clouding up and I knew darkness was coming. After watching for a while, I saw the nose of a deer who was watching me. The nose was darker with grey hair around, almost like a small target. When I saw a part of an antler, I fired on the target. Everything disappeared, so I started moving towards that target. Going real slow, I approached the spot. When I got there, I looked on the snow. The tracks were there in the snow where he turned and drooled on the snow with some red blood in the mix, but he had not fallen on the ground. I started following his tracks. I did not travel more than 100 feet when I saw him in a less dense area, slowly moving away from me. I did not want to damage the back end, so I aimed for the back of his head. He dropped right there dead. He was not the deer I had been tracking, but he was a nice six pointer.

I gutted the deer, saving the liver and the heart. When I looked at the tongue, it seemed as if the bullet had gone through the tongue and turned it into hamburger. When it was time to skin the deer, we always do the job ourselves. A deer has thick hair, and we try to keep the hair off the meat. While the deer is on the ground we cut the skin close to the head and start skinning away from the head. We put a plastic bag over the head and tie it around the neck that has already been skinned. We then hang it by the head and roll the skin down and keep the hair off the meat. All we have left to do is enjoy the meat.

Since I prefer going hunting in new areas, the next year I tried the Wallagrass Territory. I took the road going to the first Wallagrass Lake. There was good snow on the ground, but very few deer tracks. On the left side of the road, there was a good ridge, and on the right, was the Wallagrass stream. I left the road and started going up the ridge. I had not climbed very high before I started seeing tracks. After moving around, it appeared to me that the deer had their own way of traveling along the ridge and watching the hunters traveling in the road below. I slowly moved along the ridge and kept really alert. I was watching ahead and higher up the hill when suddenly, as if by magic; a huge buck pops up about 150 feet from me, to my left. He was looking directly at me as I slowly brought my rifle to my shoulder. Not wanting to damage any meat, I again picked the nose for a target. I saw him drop, but I could not see him on the ground. I slowly started moving towards where he had dropped. I could not see him as I approached the spot. I could see where he had been lying in the snow, so I looked around to find where he had gone. Finding his tracks, I looked in a path where he was heading. I saw him moving slowly up the deer trail, and I knew he was hurting. As I moved my rifle to my shoulder, I let out a little whistle. He stopped and turned his head to look at me, and I fired. He hit the ground for the last time. I cleaned him. Again, when I got to the tongue, it was greatly damaged. There, I decided my rifle was not powerful enough, so next time, I should hit lower.

    A new hunting season arrived and I was planning. Everywhere I had hunted, I had seen a great deal of tracks, rubs, and scratches, even in the snow. The decision where to hunt was made easily, since my father told me he wanted to go to his friend's camp in the Nixon area. We arrived early and after some deer talk, dad's friend told us about a swamp that they had left since there was no demand for cedar. Since I prefer hunting alone, I told my dad that he could hunt the roads around the camp while I went to visit the swamp.
    There were signs deer had spent more than one winter in there, but nothing in the fresh snow. I moved slowly, for over an hour before I had found a doe and fawn pair of tracks. I followed the tracks, but they seemed to be going as fast as I was. What I had expected happened. There stood a huge deer less than 100 feet away watching what was going on in his territory. He was almost completely hidden except for a section of his shoulder. That is where I aimed, and the deer fell down. I had been traveling in the same direction for over 2 hours. My first

thought was, how do I get this deer out of here, as I moved to examine him. Before I could reach the deer, I heard my dad whistle. I answered and went to meet him. He told me that he had been following a road made when they had cut the woods on the other side of the swamp. We both went to see and examine the deer. It was a nine point buck with an irregular rack. He really looked old. After cleaning him out and not finding any fat on him, I wondered how he could have survived the coming winter. My dad told me he would get a horse at camp to haul the deer out while I stayed in the woods with it.

After preparing the deer, I knew he had no fat and wondered how he would taste. That was my last surprise. The meat was tender and really tasty.

Reviewing this hunt, I have come to the conclusion that hunters underestimate the hearing of a deer. While traveling in new snow in that swamp, I was sure that I was noiseless, but still that deer knew everything that was going on around him. He could tell the direction and possibly even the weight and what kind of animal was in his territory. Happy hunting!

The following year, I had heard from woodcutters that a bridge had been put in on the thoroughfare between Portage Lake and Winterville Lake at Nixon Siding. This had opened a new area where deer were plentiful. Since I really enjoy visiting new territories, this was where I was heading.

I rode on a few roads where the woods had been cut two or three years back. At the end of one of those roads, I decided to walk further, beyond where I could go with my vehicle. I had not traveled more than a hundred yards when, on a hill to my left, I saw a buck as he was getting up. He was too far for a head shot, so I aimed for the shoulder. He took two or three jumps before dropping. After the cleaning, I dragged him downhill on the snow to where I could pick him up with my vehicle. He was a nice eight pointer.

Since it was still early after tagging, I decided to have him weighed. He weighed slightly over 198 pound field dressed. I was surprised because after handling him, I thought for sure he weighed more than that. It was at this time that I promised to bring another hunter with me next time.

One summer, I went fishing in the Wallagrass area on the north side of the Carter Brook. The fishing was great in the ponds created by the beaver dams. I also noticed a lot of deer signs along the brook and it seemed like the deer spent much time in the cedar swamp that reached the brook. I could hardly wait for the snow to come with that season.

When the snow came, I was ready. I moved in among the cedars and the other brush where I found much activity. I slowly moved around for a few hours, when I suddenly saw something I had not seen yet in the woods. A doe was running less than 50 feet by me and right behind her was a nice buck. The brush was quite thick and I did not have a shot, but it did not take long before the doe came back with the buck running after her. They seemed to be traveling about the same area until they disappeared going west. I waited for a while, and then I started to move slowly in the direction that they had gone. I came to a traveled trail and there was the buck, running towards me. One quick shot was all I needed. I never saw the doe again. Another season, another buck. My son Alvin was with me to help to pull him out.

My son, Alvin Theriault

The following season would be different. I had started a new job at the Fort Kent Post Office where I had to work six days a week. My friend, Lew Gervais, had invited me to join his party on a hunt to the St. Francis, Maine area on the first day of the hunting season. I could not refuse the offer to visit a new area. I made arrangements to have one day off, and I was ready to go.

We were in the woods the first minute the season opened. We all went our separate ways. I did not like the fact that there was no snow, but I moved to an area that had been cut about three years before, but was not clear-cut. After a while, I reached a side road along a swamp. There were trees that had fallen all over the road. The going was rough and I was going slow and stopping often when I saw this huge buck slowly walking to cross the road about 75 yards in front of me. I raised my rifle real easy and waited until he reached the road before pulling the trigger and he lay in the road. I could not tell where he came from, but getting him out was all I could think of. After cleaning the buck and seeing all the fat on his body, I understood why I could hardly move him. He was a ten pointer who was preparing himself for the coming rutting season.

I knew I needed help, so I put the buck in the shade and went to look for assistance at the vehicle. The rough side road I was on was about three hundred yards before it fell into a better road that took me to where we had parked. Luckily, my friend's brother happened to be taking a bite. I ate with him and I left my rifle and brought an axe. When we arrived at the buck, I used an old spruce about 3 inches in diameter and partially dried, since it had been bulldozed along the road. We tied the buck as close as we could to the pole. We knew we could not drag the deer on the ground with all the obstacles, so we would carry it. Once we had lifted the pole on our shoulders and we started moving that deer, it started swinging and almost made it impossible to stay on our feet. We then decided to use two poles with rope tied between the poles so we could put the deer on top, like a stretcher. This proved to work better. It was somewhat difficult getting it on our shoulders, but I would help him get under the poled in front, and then I could get in back. We had to rest often. We did better when it got too late to hunt and our other two partners came to help. If there is a next time, the deer will be cut up. Live and learn.

Once again the hunting season was coming. My dad liked the Nixon area where his friend had a camp. When the day arrived, we had made all the necessary arrangements. Early in the morning, I decided to walk to the camp on Beaver Brook about two miles from Route 11. About three inches of fresh snow has fallen and the weather was not real cold. I have learned to dress warm. So if I get hot, it will be all I need to slow me down.

About half way to camp, I came across a fresh track that was large enough for me. I left the road and headed in the deep woods. It was real messy, and I had to keep removing the snow from my rifle, especially the open sights.

After about an hour, the buck headed for the thick, young trees. I wondered if he had heard me and was trying to get rid of me, or maybe he was looking for company. My progress was real slow. I take a few steps and clean my rifle while I keep following the tracks. After a while, I could see what looked like a slight clearing ahead. I was bent over to keep my rifle free of snow. As I broke into that clearing, wiping the snow, my eyes met that buck face to face about 15 feet right in front of me. He spun around and headed down hill so fast that I just stood there thinking whether that was a real deer or just my imagination. I had to look at the tracks in the snow to be sure it had really happened. I got the impression while looking things over that he was expecting another buck and he had prepared to fight.

I picked up his tracks and started following him. He ran for about a quarter mile, then he walked. He soon came to where the trees weren't as thick. I was moving slowly and keeping my eyes working. I came to a place where the land was gradually going up. It was then that I could see the deer's legs at a good distance. Looking for a good target to shoot at, I laid down in the snow. The deer was facing me and I could see his chest above his front legs. That's where I put the sights and he dropped in his tracks. After the cleaning, I took my compass to find the shortest way out. The buck was an eight pointer and in good condition. The antlers were rather small for the deer's size, but I don't eat the antlers.

The coming season, a friend of mine, Camille Michaud, who worked in the woods, told me about a new area that had been opened. A bridge had been put in on the St. Francis River, below Glazier Lake, which was the border between Maine and Quebec, Canada. We had to go through Canada from Fort Kent to the bridge to get there. My friend told me there were plenty of deer in the area, and I was always eager to visit new hunting grounds.

My brother in law, Omer Dionne, and I were heading to the camp the workers were staying at. The snow was just right and we could see many deer tracks along the way. It had been wet and the road was really rough, but we reached the camp ready to hunt. The men had gone to work, so we picked a road where nobody was working. The trees were clean and we could see further than I had ever seen in the woods. We had not gone a quarter mile, when looking through the trees, way out, I could see the back of a deer. I aimed for the back and squeeze the trigger. The buck took two or three jumps before dropping. We went to him and looked the deer over. He was an eight pointer. We could hear a chainsaw not too far, so I asked my brother-in-law if he would go look for help while I cleaned the deer.

As soon as I was done this, a Canadian arrived with his horse. He got the deer out in a short time. He said he had a hard time believing I had shot that deer at that distance. He helped us load it in the trunk of our car. He would not accept any money for all his help. His name was Malcolm Oakes from Canada, and he was a very generous and helpful man.

This hunt was the shortest and easiest I had ever been on. Since there was no room to put anything else in the car, we went back home.

Edmond and buck, November 1958

The next season I planned to go back to the bridge across the thoroughfare from Portage Lake to Winterville Lake at Nixon Siding. The first time out there, I did not stay long enough to visit much of the area.

Early in the morning, with a fresh 3 inches of snow, my brother-in-law, Omer Dionne, came with me. I rode on some of the roads, but could not find any buck tracks. I decided to travel on foot in the afternoon. After about a mile, and only seeing one bobcat track, I came to a pile of bulldozed trees in a bank. I decided to send out a bleat as I stood in the road. I was surprised to get an answer immediately from the other side of that pile on the side of the road below me. I did not move or make any noise for about half an hour. I bleated again, but no answer. I slowly moved around and found where a big buck had stood. He had moved away, parallel to the road. I traveled further to where there was a small cluster of trees. I hid in there and bleated again, and again, I got an answer, but this time 5 or 6 deer answered. I was surprised that each of their bleats was different. I waited until it was time to stop hunting. I went to see what had happened. They were bedded down. When I arrived, they got up and walked into the swamp beyond, saying goodbye in their bleating way. There was no meat that year since that was the last day of the season.

My plan for the hunting season was simple; I would hunt in the Wallagrass area. It was the closest to home, and there was something else I had noticed. When I clean a deer, the fat inside the body sticks to my knife and my hands, especially around the fingernails. In some cases, it was hard to wipe off. What I had noticed was that the more it sticks to your hands, the more it would stick to the inside of your mouth when you ate it. I really don't know what caused it, but I found out that deer from the Wallagrass area were less sticky.

I always prefer hunting with snow, so I hunt almost at the end of the season. That season found me walking on the road to the first Wallagrass Lake with about five inches of snow on the ground. With tracks to look at, I could image what goes on with the animals.

After walking about a mile, I left the road and started climbing the ridge on the left side. On my right was the Wallagrass Stream. The ridge was not too steep, but I had to slow down to keep from overheating.

I had not seen anything so far, but the visibility was good. The woods did not have brushes to obstruct your vision. As I slowly moved up the slope, I came across two sets of deer tracks running away from me. I looked at the tracks and wondered if I was the one that jumped them. I looked to see where they could be going. After a good 15 minutes of just looking, I saw a nice big buck in the distance, walking at a fast pace up the slope to hit the tracks of the two deer I had been following. When he came to the tracks, he stopped for a short moment and with his nose almost in the tracks, he headed towards me. He was going in the wrong direction. I thought it could be that he could not tell which way the tracks were going. I raised my rifle, but since he was coming towards me with his nose to the tracks, I waited. When he came to less than 50 feet from me, he just seemed to freeze. He was looking right at me, and he looked exactly like a statue as I pulled the trigger. He fell in his tracks.

The law on fluorescent orange had been passed, and I did not want to take my vest off. I am for whatever makes hunting safer, and I don't believe it makes any difference to the deer.

November 1957

This season I was going back to the Wallagrass area. There was more snow than usual, but there would be wood cutting on that road to the Third Lake. I knew the road would be kept open during the hunting season, so there would be no chance of getting stuck in there. My hunting partner was my brother-in-law, Omer Dionne.

After riding for some time and not seeing any signs, we took a break, ate lunch, and started heading back. We came to where a good size buck had crossed the road, coming from the direction of the Carter Brook. He was headed up to higher country. The track was fresh, so I decided to go after that buck. The snow was about eight inches deep, making the going more difficult. I followed slowly up the hill. As I got higher, I could see much further. The snow was keeping the noise down, but I only saw the buck when he moved against the white snow background. I pulled the trigger. When it was far, I try to hit in the shoulder. He took a few jumps before he dropped. In all my hunting, I have never tried to get closer for an easier shot, and I move real slow. My brother-in-law heard the shot. When he arrived, the deer was ready to be dragged downhill, which was not too hard. The hunt and the season were over.

Edmond & Mike Gagnon were both lucky!

This year I would hunt in the Nixon area where my father's friend had a camp by the Beaver Brook. There was a good snow and a lot of tracks, but there was something missing. Where I use to have no problem finding fawn tracks, I had trouble finding any that year. That made me really sad because I knew that without fawns, the wonderful hunting years were numbered. I promised myself that the next year, I would do more riding around just to verify what I suspected.

That year, there seems to be no shortage of bucks. I found a bunch of trees where tracks were leading into. It was impossible to go in there and expect to be able to see anything. I stayed at a distance where there was a somewhat clear area. I could hear branches breaking once or twice. I thought maybe if I laid down in the snow, I could probably be able to see more. It was getting late in the day, but I waited. The first thing that I saw was a nice set of antlers coming out of the brush. He kept his head low as he came out. He was coming right at me when I fired. He took off towards me not more than two feet from the ground I was on. I was sure he was going to run over me so I rolled over, and just in time. His tracks were right where I had been laying. I brought him home the next day.

This hunting season found me in the Wallagrass area. The snow was about six inches deep. It had been snowing and the trees were loaded and the wind was gusty. Every gust of wind brought enough snow down so that you could not see anything. My brother-in-law, Omer Dionne, was with me. On the road to First Lake, we found three fresh sets of tracks crossing the road. Vehicles had traveled on the road, so we could tell that two sets of tracks were more pointed and made by does and on the other set, the point was more rounded and made by a good size buck. (It is hard to tell the sex of the deer if you can't see the front end of the track. To tell how fresh tracks are, you can pass your hand through the snow where the track is. Snow hardens after is has been disturbed, and the colder it is the faster it hardens.)

I decided to follow those deer since they did not seem to be in any hurry. After getting about one hundred yards from the road, the deer started feeding on some young trees and plants that grew in some old wood cutting. I noticed that whenever a gust of wind came, it knocked snow off the trees. I could not see anything in front of me as long as the wind lasted. What I did was wait for the wind to start making noise and bringing the snow down before I moved. After about half an hour, when the wind stopped, I was surprised to see this odd looking doe not more than fifty feet in front of me. The doe had no ears and I decided to take her. I remembered hearing old hunters telling how that could happen and I was curious to check it out. The doe could have been about a year and a half old and in good condition. She had not produced fawn yet. What the hunters had told me was that during harsh winters, it was the does bearing young that were likely not to survive. When the next rutting season came around, there was a shortage of females and a surplus of bucks. Some bucks would run after females that were too young. After these young females became exhausted and could go no further, they just laid down on the ground. The bucks tried to get them on their feet to no avail. They would get so frustrated that they ate the young female's ears.

Here I had a doe that fitted that story. The ears had not been clean cut and the jagged edges, about one inch from the head, were well healed. It was good eating.

This year, I would try to find out what the coyotes were doing to the deer herd in Northern Maine. My son, Alvin, who trapped to pay his way through college, reported that some of the furs were being damaged by coyotes. Other trappers were saying the same.

I could arrange to be off work whenever I wanted. So on the very first snow; I went to the area of Little and Big California where there use to be a lot of deer. On the roads, wherever I found deer tracks, I also found coyote tracks. I traveled roads all day long and it was the same everywhere. Doe tracks, but no fawn.

I went riding again late in the season, and if anything, it was even worse. In Northern Maine, the winters had always been tough. We had real bad winters, but the deer herd always quickly recovered. Now with the buck's only law, the herd didn't seem to improve.

I have not hunted deer for thirty-five years. I tried hunting deer twice in thirty years, and I felt it was time wasted. I am writing to let the hunters of today know what hunting was like at that time. Now, I say again, if you have no fawns, in about five years, you have no deer. I trapped coyotes, but I could not afford to continue. So now, except for three or four moose hunts, I have not hunted or trapped for thirty-five years.

Chapter 3
Hector Long Story

    This story was told to me by a friend, Hector Long, who was hunting at Gilbert Godin's camp at Nixon on the Beaver Brook. He had hunted the morning I arrived and had shot a ten point buck. He said he was following this buck's tracks in about eight inches of snow. He had been following his tracks for a couple of hours when he spotted the deer's head with antlers between trees at close range. He shot, and the deer fell right there. He slowly approached the deer. When he was close, he was sure the deer was dead, so he leaned his rifle against a tree and started moving toward him, when he noticed the deer was getting up. He did not want to lose that deer, so he wrapped his arms in the antlers and the buck started pushing him around. After a while, the deer must have been getting tired. When the buck pushed him against small trees, he was breathing hard and stopped pushing. My friend freed one hand and got his knife and cut an artery. The buck kept pushing and bleeding until he fell to his knees. After what seemed to be a long time, the deer's rear end went down. He was dead. My friend and his brother dragged him out. After examining the head, he saw where his jaw was broken. He promised that he would never do that again, even after going through that ride without getting hurt.

    I knew where the buck had been dragged out, so I went to see how that place looked. It was worse than my friend had described. The snow was trampled in a large area with broken branches and damaged smaller trees. The blood was in one spot mainly. I certainly would not want to be involved in that type of exercise.

Chapter 4

Tips and Things About Hunting

One hunting season, with my third son, Galen, we went hunting by Third Sly Brook Lake. There was no snow on the ground and when we came to a well traveled deer trail about 300 feet from the lake, I told Galen we would try something new. There was an old stump with small trees around it near the trail. I told Galen to set himself on the stump so he could watch the trail to the south and I would circle away from the lake for about a mile and come back walking slowly north on the trail towards him. About an hour later, I was slowly heading north on the trail, when I heard a rifle shot in front me. I thought that was an easy hunt. I walked to where Galen was sitting. Coming to him, I asked what had happened. He said he had seen this nice buck and taken a shot. Trouble was, the buck was coming from the north and he is right handed, so he did not want to move since the buck was so close. He slowly twisted and shot left handed and missed. The buck must have heard him break branches when he set up and just came to investigate what was going on.

DRAGGING AND LOADING A MOOSE OR DEER WITH ANTLERS

You can drag more easily by dragging the animal back legs first, so you will not have to worry about the antlers getting caught and damaged. You can move the animal before removing the entrails if you do not want to leave them in the road or where the animal died. I have heard it is not good public relations if you leave the entrails where they can be seen from the road.

You want to tie the rope with knots that are easy to tie and untie. This is how I tie the rope to the legs: I tie the hind legs together with a slip knot above the knees, then I make two half hitches below the knees, ending underneath the legs.

With a cow, I make the slip knot around the neck with one half hitch around the nose and underneath. When you star dragging, you are lifting the hind legs or the head to help pass over obstacles on the ground. The tie to whatever is pulling can be made with two half hitches as shown.

DRAGGING ANIMAL TO ROAD

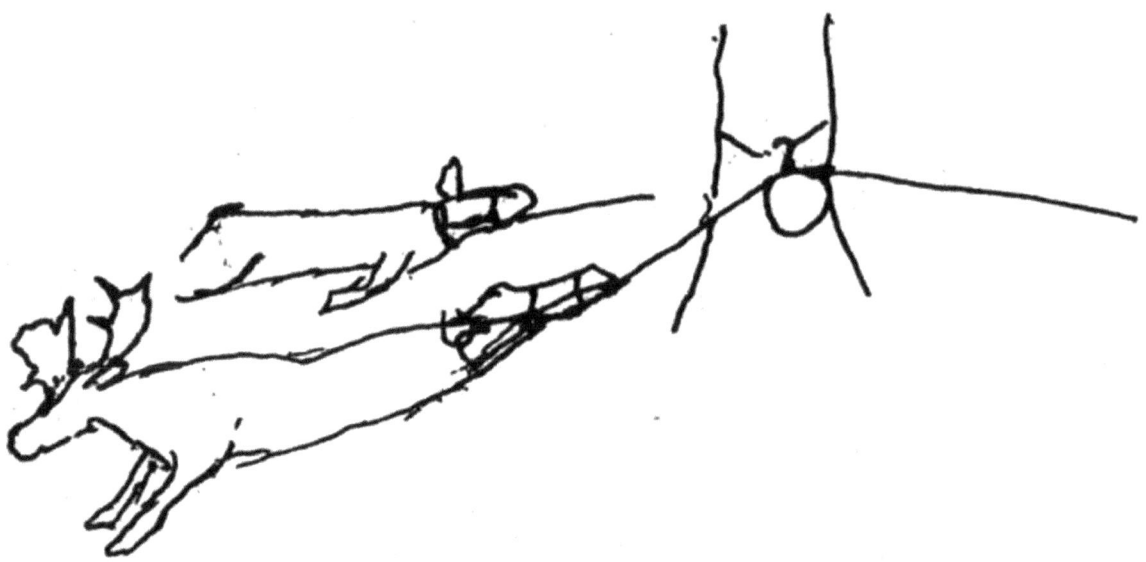

Tie to drag animal with antlers: one slip knot above the knees, two half hitches below the knees.

If pulley is needed, pulley can be tied to tree or stump or hitch of second pick-up.

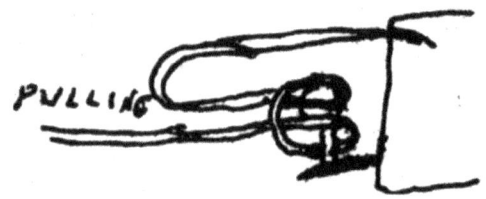

TYING ROPE TO TRAILER HITCH

Important knot that is easy to tie and to untie without cutting rope. Standing behind pick-up near hitch, make a loop about two feet long and hold in right hand, with left hand take bottom of loop and bring up to be held under right thumb. Left hand, adjust two hitches to be dropped over ball of hitch. Make sure pulling rope is on bottom.

LOADING ANIMAL ON A TRAILER

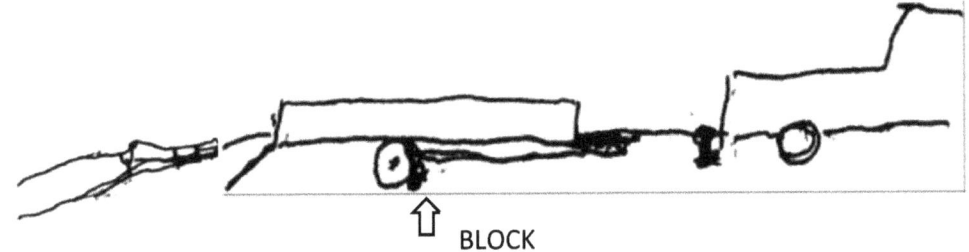

⇧ BLOCK

LOADING ANIMAL ON A PICK-UP

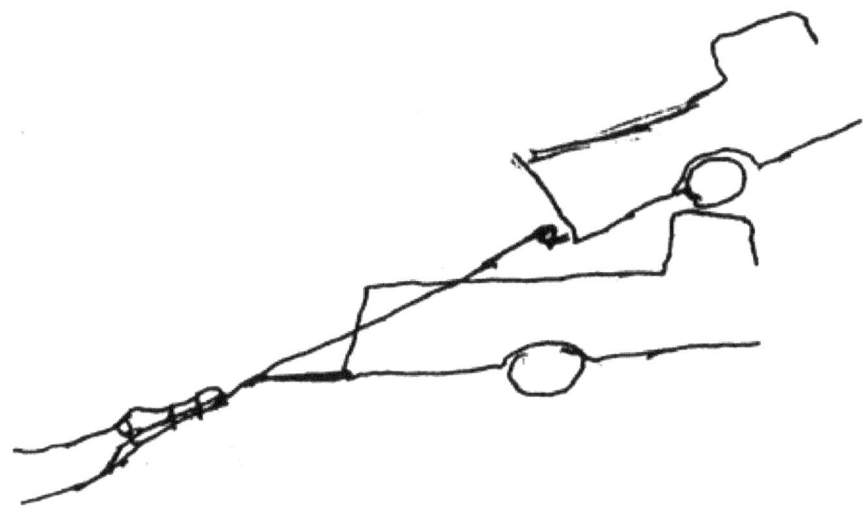

Open tail-gate, pass rope over the tail-gate and side of pick-up, have second pick-up pull animal in. If second pick-up is not available, tie the rope to a tree at an angle, and back against rope.

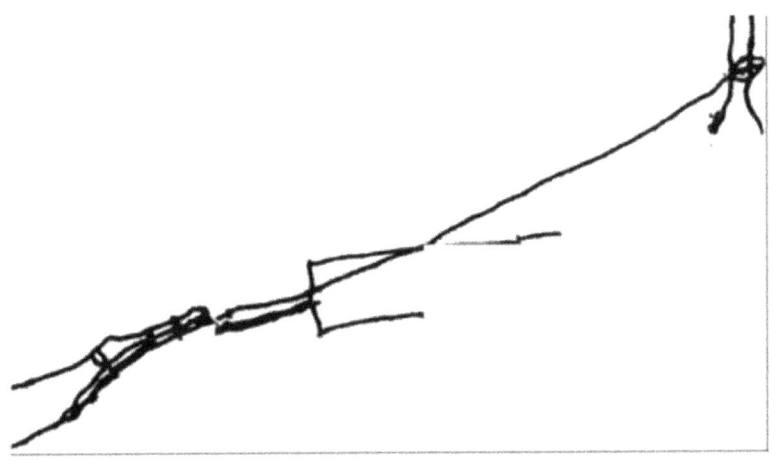

Move slowly. Second hunter should stand near open tail gate to watch that all goes well.

DEER FIGHTING ARENA

    I have seen many areas where bucks have been fighting, with blood on the snow and holes made by antlers in the ground. The land almost looked like it had been plowed. But the number of bucks involved was small.

    One day I had gone hunting west of Eagle Lake. There was about six inches of snow on the ground when I came to an area on the side of a ridge with a low dip in the center. As I moved in there on the track of a buck, I found so may buck tracks that I could not count them. There were many spots where the bucks had been fighting and when I circled this area I found the bucks had been coming and leaving from every direction. All the tracks had been made not long before I arrived. After going around this area a second time trying to decide which direction would be better to go, I stopped to look this area over. In my mind I could see some of these bucks fighting in the dip in the land, while the others watched the fight, and sometimes going to join in. I could not imagine the day would come when deer would have almost disappeared in Northern Maine. On this day, I decided to leave this area undisturbed.

DIFFERENT WAYS OF HUNTING AND CALLING BUCKS

These methods have been passed on to me by old hunters and my father, who learned from Native Americans.

1. BLEATING: I have tried it with success by imitation, but I have not tried deer callers with a rubber band.

2. RUBBING: Breaking branches and rubbing antlers against small trees the way bucks remove the dead velvet from their antlers. I have never tried it.

3. RATTLING: Rubbing and hitting two antlers together to represent fighting bucks.

4. You can use a dry hardwood stick about two feet long and 1 inch in diameter to hit on the root of a standing tree three or four times to imitate a doe calling for company. Repeat about every twenty minutes.

5. Pouring water on dry leaves can attract a buck.

6. SCRAPES: Bucks have travel ways they follow throughout their territory. At certain spots, they will paw the ground to leave marks of their area. These scrapes can be three to four feet in diameter. The bucks urinate inside of these scrapes and visit them about every three days. Does visit these scrapes and also urinate in them. When the buck does his rounds, he checks and if the doe is approaching the time to be bred, he will take off after her. This is a good spot to hide and watch.

7. All animals travel and feed before and after a storm.

8. TRACKING: Is my favorite method. I try to understand what the deer is doing and why. Of course, I combine other methods.

9. A method that I really like is an old one. You cut a piece of skin that contains the dark brown gland on the back legs of a doe. You tie these pieces of skin to the back of your boots so they will drag on the ground. You walk around

where you want to hide and going deeper in the woods, and coming out to where you will be hiding. You go where you have seen scrapes if possible. If these skins containing the glands are not available, you can use strong materials and put doe scents on them. If you use doe glands, be sure to wash your hands and your hunting knife, so you will not contaminate the meat. Don't be surprised if a hungry coyote shows up.

10. Do not try to call a deer that snorted or whistled, by imitation. When a deer whistles, that is a danger signal being sent to warn other deer in the area.

Whatever method you use, stop and wait as soon as you hear or see anything that can be caused by a buck.

DEER TRAPPED BY BEARS

A bridge had been built between the First and Second Wallagrass Lakes. I decided to go hunting in the area to the south of the lakes even if there was no snow. The road was rough, so I crossed the bridge on foot. It looked like the cutting was finished. I had been slowly moving through the cuttings heading west for two or three hours. There were plenty of deer signs everywhere. At one spot, where there seemed to be a trail heading back almost in the same direction I had been coming from. I decided to go see where the trail was coming from. I had not traveled a hundred feet when I jumped a good buck that started running fast and not coming up more than two feet above the ground. He was heading down hill and I missed my hip-shot. The buck had been bedded down and he let me go by the first time, but when I started coming back, he took off. I was getting far from my vehicle, so I decided to come back by going through the dead waters above the Second Lake.

Fishermen had told me that trout fishing was good after the shallow water of the Second Wallagrass Lake started to warm up in the summer. I wanted to see what it looked like. I started looking to find a way to get through the thick swampy land. I found a well traveled deer trail that was used to go for drinking water and cooling off. This trail passed through small cedars so thick that following this trail was the only way you could go. As I moved along, I came to a clearing next to the trail. The clearing was about twenty-five feet in diameter with bones, mostly pieces of skulls, all over, and bear dropping of all ages everywhere. I examined everything and was surprised to find that some of those bear piles contained nothing but deer hair. I looked around to see how the bears were catching the deer. I saw where the bears would hide, and when the deer came in single file, he would grab the first one who had no place to go since the trail was so narrow with the side cedars acting as a fence. I never could figure out why trees were not growing in that clearing.

It was time to leave, so I took the trail and when I came to the dead waters, I crossed on an old beaver dam and walked on the north side of the lake to where I had left my car on a good road.

BEAR NEST

It was at the end of November that I brought my three sons, Alvin, Brian, and Galen, hunting. The only area that had snow was south of Ashland, going towards Mapleton, so that is where we went. We parked the car on an abandoned woods road about one mile from Haystack Mountain. Four inches of snow had been on the ground for three days and we had no problem finding deer tracks. We split up and went on our own way. It was not long before I hit three fresh tracks that showed a good size buck. I followed these tracks. The first thing the deer did was cross the highway and head south. After about an hour and a half of tracking, it started to snow. I worried about what my sons would do, so I decided to head back. I checked my compass to find the shortest way to the highway.

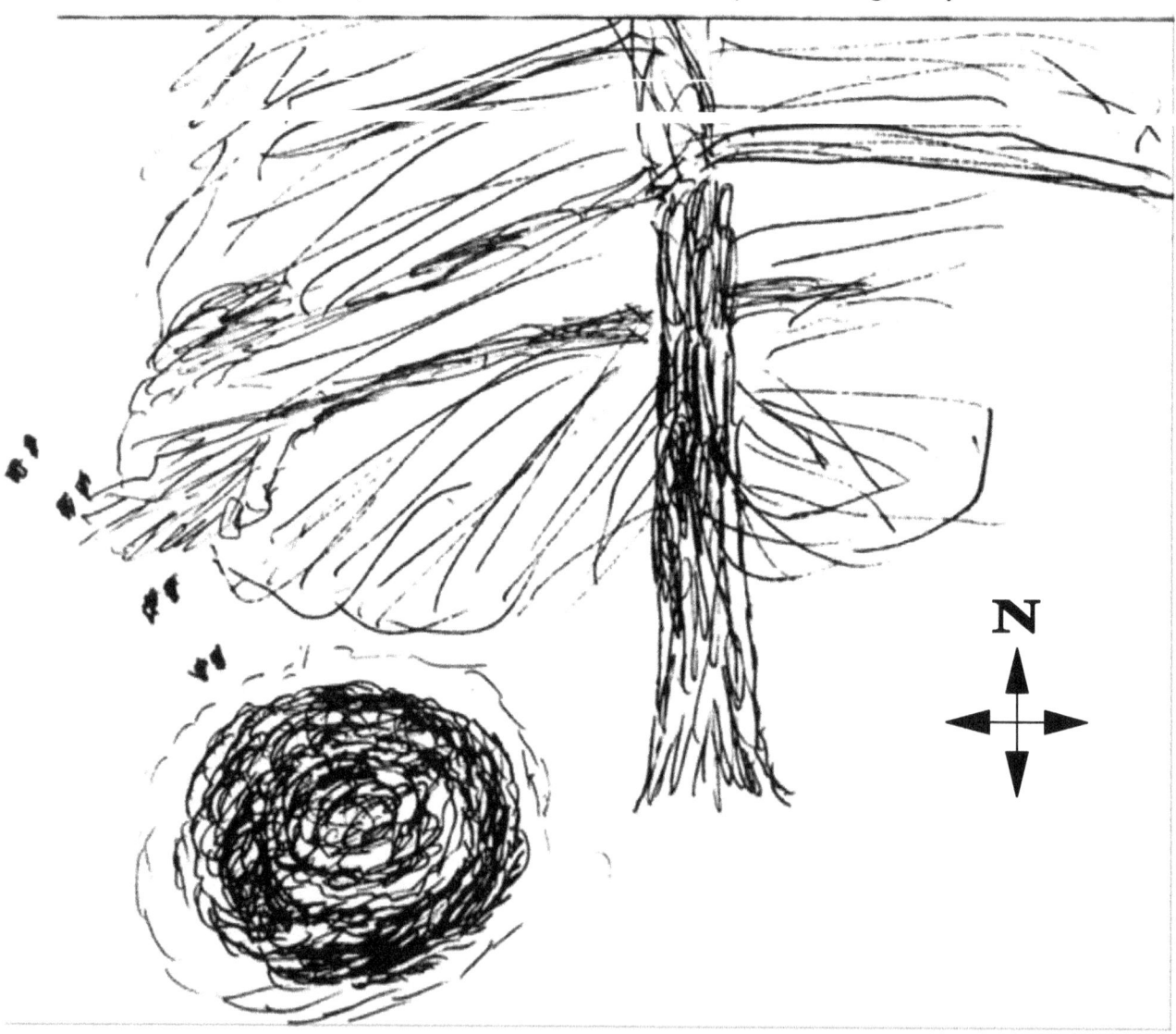

I was coming from the south, when the bear in the nest took off in the northwest direction. I was about seventy-five feet from him, and in a very short time, that bear was moving very fast, leaving snow dust behind him. I fired once and he had disappeared making much noise, breaking branches that were left on the ground when the wood had been cut five or six years before. There was about three to four inches of snow, and I followed to see if I had hit him. When you follow tracks looking for blood, you have to keep looking back at your tracks also. A drop of warm blood falling on snow can sink and disappear. But when you step on it, a red spot will appear in your track. Finding no blood, I returned to where the bear had been sleeping. Old woodsman had told me of findings bear nests in winter under large fir trees, and here I was looking at one. Since I had no camera, I will describe what I saw. It looked as if the bear had scraped everything on the ground into a pile under this large fir tree, and then he climbed on top and worked the pile into a nest about six feet in diameter and then had curled in it. The snow had been on the ground for three days and was where it fell all around the nest. There were no tracks all around except those where the bear left. The outside of the nest was frozen solid and the inside was wet where the bear had been sleeping. The thickness of the top of the nest was about six inches all around. Since the inside was not frozen, you could tell it was material scraped off the ground. I left and when I got back to the car, my sons were waiting for me. It was snowing and they were worried about me. We were happy to go home. After getting home, I started thinking of the bear. He was not worried about the cold. The big tree would keep some of the snow off of him. It was at that time that I remembered my father telling me that in some areas, fir trees tended to be hollow. He showed me how by tapping on the tree with the head of his ax, he could tell about how hollow it was. The wood cutters did not want to waste time cutting these frozen fir trees with an ax if it was not good, so they left the tree to grow. The bear, looking for a large tree, selected a large fir.

My friend, Melvin Godin, came to see me to see if I could help him. He had been hunting deer with his son and coming back they received a great surprise. It was at the end of November with about six inches of snow on the ground. They decided to take a short-cut since it was getting late. When they approached some trees that had been blown down, a large bear stood up right in front of them. They shot the bear, and he took a few steps away from them and fell dead. Before they even moved, a second bear came out and they shot it. When a third bear came out, he ran to the first dead bear, where he stopped for about a second and then ran down hill as fast as he could. They had a large sow and one of her large cubs. The cubs must have been almost two years old. I told Melvin that I would help track the bear. I followed the running bear for over an hour and he never slowed down. I wanted to see what the third bear had done and where the bears had decided to spend the winter. So I came back to look at the place where the bears were sleeping. It seemed the bears had crawled under three trees that had been blown down about two to three feet off the ground. The trees were about four to five inches in diameter and did not offer much shelter. I asked myself, how long does it take before the bears start their sleep for the winter, and do they depend on the snow that will fall to insulate them from the cold? Maybe a pregnant sow looks for a better den to have her young.

Chapter 5

A Moose Hunt

My daughter, Aileen, had the moose permit and I was the subpermittee. Philip Boucher, my son-in law, was driving his pick-up truck on Golden road. Aileen spotted the bull moose on our right, and Phil pulled over on the right and stopped. I took my 308 rifle and slowly got out and moved to the back of the pick-up where the moose couldn't see me. I loaded the rifle and moved forward and shot the moose in the neck at about two hundred feet. The moose dropped with his head under him. The trees had been cut and the terrain was real rough. As I slowly moved through, I kept watching the moose. I could see his neck had a bloody spot where the bullet had entered and the moose was still breathing. It was at that time that the moose pulled up his head and in seconds, he was going full speed towards me. I fired once as he neared me and a second time after he had passed. He was so close, I was afraid he could reach me with his antlers. I could not believe he could move that fast in this rough territory. His momentum landed him right in the road. Phil told my daughter I was shooting like "The Rifleman". My daughter came out of the pick-up with her camera and took a picture as I was checking to make sure he was dead.

1991

We emptied the moose and as soon as we were done, an elder couple drove up and stopped to look at the moose. I asked him if he had a trailer hitch. He had, and was happy to help us load the moose. We loaded the moose as described previously in this book, and went home.

On examination, we found three bullet holes in the neck of the moose, and none had gone through. The 308 was not strong enough. After that incident, I used a 30-06.

Chapter 6

Philippine Hunt

One day, while overseas, a party of about eight took two jeeps and went hunting in Northern Louzon of the Philippines. I was very surprised to find that the ground in those mountains was made of old sea corals. We did see deer, wild ponies, water buffaloes and calf, many monkeys, and a large type of lizard about five or six feet long running away from us.

Only one member of our party killed a deer, which looked like the deer back home. We cooked and ate steak and brought the remainder back to base for the others.

Chapter 7

Porky

While hunting for rabbits east of Highway 161 and north of Daigle Pond, I started hearing a strange noise. I moved to investigate. As I approached a steep hillside that had this huge rock sticking out of the ground, I saw this pile of what looked like wood pellets stacked against the bottom of the rocky outcropping. It was about ten feet high and ten feet wide at ground level. There was a ledge in the rock above and the rock had cracks. That could have been caused by frost. I saw the porcupines and was making the noise on the ledge. It was obvious this was a safe haven for these animals. All they had to do was stick their heads in one of the cracks, about a foot, and wait. The cracks did not seem to go deep, but from the manure pile, this haven had been used for a number of years.

About ten years later, I took a friend of mine who wanted to see that place. There was about six inches of snow on the ground. I wanted to see how they survived in the winter. They had a trail going to the tree they were feeding on. They ate the bark and killed the tree. I was surprised not to see more dead trees in the area.

Old hunters had told me the porcupine is about the only animal a man can outrun and kill with a stick. That is why they call it the friend of a lost person. I decided to bring one home and try it. I shot a smaller one with my 22 and skinned it. My mother who was a good cook took care of it. I firmly believe she did not want me to bring any more home. The meat was tender and juicy, but without taste. She did not use anything but water on it.

There was another place porcupines were using that looked like an abandoned foxhole. It looked like it was a female expecting. It seemed like all she had to do if unexpected guests showed up was turn her backside to close the entrance.

Chapter 8

Partridges

In the 1930's, when you went hunting for rabbits and partridges, you would see how partridges survived the cold winter nights. Now you don't hear about it, maybe because partridges are scarce. When there was snow on the ground and a cold night was expected, the partridges would fly around and find an area that was opened enough and not traveled. The bird would dive in the snow and block the entrance with snow and spend the night under the snow where it was not freezing cold. They were in no hurry to get out in the morning since they had eaten buds, especially from the white and yellow birch family, which are common. When you walked on snowshoes in the morning, you could see where the bird had entered the snow. You could tell if the bird had been surprised and left by the marks left by the wing feathers in the snow, as it took off. If it was still in the hole, you could slowly approach and place your snowshoe on top of the hole, preventing its escape. It is quite a nerve-racking experience when you step on or near a hole by accident as the bird is coming out. They make a surprising noise taking off that close. In the woods, the birds choose a place to dive where they can also escape. Some woodsmen have told me they had found where the snow had so hardened that the bird died because it could not get out. I have never found a case like that, but I have found where foxes had eaten them near the hole. I don't even know if the bird was dead or alive.

Chapter 9

A Chilling Warning

All outdoors people, especially beaver trappers who like to go on ice early in the season, need to be careful. Ice on lakes and small ponds can be dangerous. There are springs and fast moving water that can slow ice from forming. Beavers keep an area open in front of their lodge.

One season, my son Brian and I went to set beaver traps after four of five inches of snow had fallen. We brought our hound dog for exercise. The dog smelled everything everywhere while we were beginning to set traps. When the dog passed in front of the lodge, he broke through the ice and went in. Her could swim, but he could not get out. The water must be cold to form ice, so we moved in where we thought the ice was stronger. I sent Brian crawling ahead of me since he was lighter. When he reached the dog, he helped him by grabbing his collar and pulling until he could climb on the ice. The dog was young, but he knew instinctively what he had to do. When we pull a soaking wet beaver from under the ice, we roll it in the snow to dry it. That is exactly what the dog did until he felt he was dry enough and he continued nosing around.

One year, I climbed on a dam to check the ice. There was about 4 inches of ice, so I made a pole set. I decided to go around and make a blind set at the open inlet. All went well and I left. The next day was milder and I decided to check the traps since I was passing nearby. The pole set was still in place, but the ice where I had traveled to go around was all gone, including the inlet. I managed to reach the second trap and picked it up. There was a muskrat in it. I learned that the ice thickness on a dam is not all the same. Sometimes the snow on the ice will insulate it from the cold.

You do not want to travel on a dam on snowshoes. If you break through it, it will be hard or impossible to get out. I always take my snowshoes off or open the buckle that keeps me from sliding my foot out of the snowshoe. Getting out of snowshoes under water is next to impossible. After you get out of the water, soaking wet, you only have a short period of time on a cold morning to get out of your wet clothes before they freeze and make it almost impossible to move.

Test the ice often, especially if you are the first one going on it.

Hunting Tools

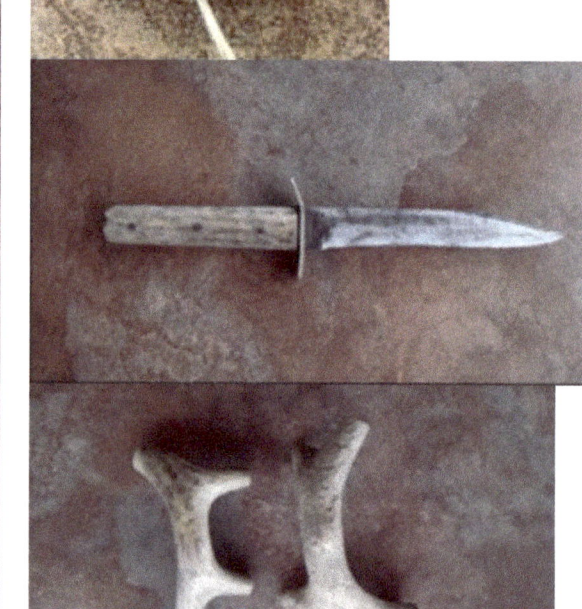

Venison Mincemeat Pie

Edmond's wife, Joan (Pelletier) Theriault, wanted to include the recipe for her husband's favorite venison mincemeat pie.

Filling for Two Pies:
2 cups cooked and chopped deer meat (neck preferred)
4 cups peeled and chopped apples
½ cup chopped raisins
¼ cup brown sugar
¼ cup molasses
¼ cup orange marmalade
¼ cup grape juice
¼ cup cider
1 tablespoon lemon juice
¼ teaspoon nutmeg
¼ teaspoon cinnamon
¼ teaspoon salt

Mix ingredients well in a pot and slowly cook on the stove until consistency is right for pie filling.

Pie Crust:
3 cups flour
1 ½ cup Crisco
1 teaspoon sugar
1 tablespoon vinegar
1 egg
 ¼ cup water

About the Author:

Edmond Theriault was born on March 22, 1923 in Fort Kent, Maine. Edmond started going in the woods with his father when he was too young to even use tools. His father was cutting firewood and Edmond would bring the lunch. Everyone had work to do.

At that time, many children did not want to go to school. Edmond was the only male in his class to graduate from high school.

It was about that time that his grandfather, Joseph Babin, came home and told his daughter, Edmond's mother, that maybe she should not have so many children. His mother, who was proud of her large family, asked him who would defend us and our freedom if we didn't have children. She said she would rather have her sons fighting for her than anyone else. All the boys in the family served in the military during World War II. Eli joined the Army Air Corps and went to flight school and was made a B-17 pilot. Alban joined the Infantry and spent one year and a half as a platoon leader in Europe. Edmond joined the Army Air Corps and went to flight school and spent twenty-two months in the Pacific Theater as a B-17 pilot. Alire (Pete) joined the Air Force. Donald served for over thirty years in the Air Force.

After discharge from the military, Edmond returned to Fort Kent, Maine. He married Joan Pelletier, and together they raised a family of eleven children. Edmond worked for over thirty years for the United States Post Office.

Edmond began the craft of snowshoe making when he was young. His father had made snowshoes, and Edmond continued and perfected the art. His son, Brian, collaborated with his father to keep that old tradition of snowshoe making alive.

Together, they published a book, *Leaving Tracks, A Maine Tradition*. All the steps of traditional snowshoe making are included.

www.ingramcontent.com/pod-product-compliance
Lightning Source LLC
Chambersburg PA
CBHW042229010526
44113CB00046B/2932